ONOMATOPOEIA

poems by

Hunter Grey

Finishing Line Press
Georgetown, Kentucky

ONOMATOPOEIA

ACKNOWLEDGMENTS

Special thanks to:

Rick Jackson, for always being the guy

&

Alexis Olson, for designing the cover of this book, and for the million other
things

Publisher: Leah Huete de Maines
Editor: Christen Kincaid
Cover Art and Design: Alexis Olson
Author Photo: Emily Hobbs

Order online: www.finishinglinepress.com
also available on amazon.com

Author inquiries and mail orders:
Finishing Line Press
PO Box 1626
Georgetown, Kentucky 40324
USA

Contents

PELVIS

Listen. I ATARI'd mine and you ATARI'd yours. It was
post-war time and things were different. Canaries built up
incredible tolerances to all sorts of otherwise lethal junk.
Dale Earnhardt had long hair. And I'm not here to tell you who
you should or shouldn't let into your heart. That

stuff never got me right anyway. Left me stiff as a board on the day
after Christmas. Lacking all juice. Impertinent for chickadees. What
was that one song that everybody loved? I loved it too. I
called it mine. And so it was. I called it ours and so
we were. In July. Where the fence is rotten with honeysuckle and the
    field

purples in the summer evening. The good news
is that there are no secrets anymore. The rituals worked. As
rituals. Even when the incense was gone and all we had left to burn
were woven strands of our own hair. In the end it reeked
even more like angels. So silly we couldn't see it coming.

SLEDGE

A cow lowed so loud that it split the river. Made
good time. A second summer. Fruits and basket cases
got all the attention. Dressed in fines of regal genitalia. Sometimes
slacks. Anyway, what could any of us do? Afterall we were

transfixed. Suspicion being the least of that which was aroused. But
    the most potable.
And the rest is history. Un-
reflected. Full of haunts. Quiet. The brass and woodwinds
are warming their instruments. The drummers' brushes itching.

PLEASURE BOATS

I was surprised. By the early air not because it was early but
because it was still humming off vestigial midnight fairy-circle
conspiracies. All hush-hush. Not about getting even. Though not

not about that. The rough stuff. That is. The real Jim Crow stuff. Goats
can eat poison all day long. Snakes play dead like coils
of coyote shit while sun breeds flies by immaculate conception.
   Miracles

of evolution. All. A Dixieland stampede. That is. Amid
the old bone China. It's the kids. They'll grow
chambered stomachs all on their own. And in their own sweet time
   too

UNTITLED

Out in the empty field some wild strawberries
aren't even strawberries. I wasn't there
when they called my ticket at the raffle. Had to scrape by
on the wanton heads of strawberries. During the Strawberry Parade

every street is renamed Strawberry. The Strawberry Queen
will be crowned today at 3pm on the steps at the corner
of Strawberry and Strawberry. On Jupiter the air
is so dense that when it rains it rains 24 carat

encyclopedias. There are no strawberries on Jupiter. Nobody
there has ever even heard of one. They call them encyclopedias.
    Their teeth
are made of glass and they go to church on Tuesdays.
They have no way of knowing how backward they really are.

DIESEL 40

The trick is to picture everybody naked. Snow makes
children of us all. The song went like this. Now Peter and Paul
and Josiah went running backward up Mount Moriah. They turned

their wine to turpentine. They ate
fistfuls of sand. I'm getting ahead of myself. Suffice to say that
mistakes were made. We were born too soon and covered all over

in fine, fine hairs. The mountain let us into her side. Sweetly.
 At school we learned about something called
The Diet of Worms. And how sulfur can flower in the presence

of some strange insoluble holy water. All in all good stuff. And further
    proof that
nothing is what it might be. *God be*
at your table. Give us the high sign when it's safe to come out.

PERFECT-BOUND

One day
starlings go on killing time
in empty baseball diamonds.

One day
papa rhymes with *soda*
and it makes the heart glad.

One day
something Grecian
happens.

One day
the daisy in the window finally says *Enough!*
to my tepid anthropomorphisms.

One day
Fate shows little interest in where
the signs are pointing.

One day
even though it wasn't supposed to
it rains.

MONOFILAMENT

Somebody put something archaic in my denominator.
Winsome as a winsome drapery. Busted as an old leather shoe

dipped in bronze. Turns out funny in the end that
all Booth really wanted to do was make a birdhouse out of Old Abe's

transatlantic prow. Having as he had then more birds
than boxes to put them in. Nobody buries their secret treasures

in their own backyard. That was the easy part. Inevitably so.
That was the part covered in deadly ribbons and bows.

MARL

One night the coyotes came and left tracks in the coop
and a certain type of flower called
blood-spattered chicken feathers. Something had to be done so
we all threw dice and watched them settle down
watery and fertile as baby teeth. Haphazardly

the Masons came round hard and knocking on doors. Said that
somebody had stolen the corn from out of their hats. *Scatter!*
somebody yelled. And we all scattered. The next day
I was in the hospital with a broken leg. It didn't work right.
Somebody brought me a bouquet of *blood-spattered chicken feathers.*
   That

was the first of July and the townspeople
were happy. The sky spread out overhead like a picnic blanket.
Atonements were made without knowing for what. Just so
that like a bed they can be made. And made. All month
I had to eat sour grapes to keep from smiling.

EARTHWORKS

It's OK that we never got to be what
we wanted to be. Or all that serious. I wanted to be
a starting pistol at the '76 Summer Games. That was a long time ago.
   And
Charles got it worst but that's only because he got it

first. So much for soup. The plane touches down and
a conveyer spits out bags from nowhere. Not mine. Not me
so much as us. I'm speaking for us. There was a bum
in an earlier draft of this thing but I didn't know where to put him. So

I'll put him here. Where he crosses against the light
to display his talent for telekinesis. To show that he
too can stop cars with his mind. Toot their horns. It was funny. We all
were funny. We had to be.

BASIN

I ate of Elvis and drank of Elvis and became erudite
and calm. It was a golden opportunity. A tender loin. When
the wind came down out of upland countries
it was to tell us all about the new and interesting ways
we could wear our socks. And there were thousands. Glacier herds

only then were learning how to walk as down in the valley's curtain I
sat beside a heap of bricks the sun was teething on.
Handfuls of snakes kept themselves pretty busy that day. Decking
the bushes with strings of thorn
and warming their bellies by death ray as if by a fire.

HONEYMOON

Foxes go out with frost tipping on their boots. To ransack
sleeping dens and leave their tracks not hither nor yon on slopes
of the blue hill. Fieldstones wait out in the empty field. To be
harvested. And the hearts of the dead are turning ripe again.
Shouldering up dirt in the bed as tuber. And radish. The spade

weathers the night standing on its head. Moony by the shed. Inside
the wine pulls no tricks and it's our bones that take turns at
fouling up Jacob's Ladder. We make faces at the dark. We screw
our brains out and then lie there and listen. Windchimes. Seaming
the night back together. Lead veins in a stained-glass window.

HERON

Great big windows. Something about noble gas
condensed as the grass blade and pine needle tap and die
on high noon's lean gable. Like it were
God's honest truth the hammer in the sunk piano

hammers on its designated wire. The fountain goes out
by degrees. And seeing as how the blue
high-water marks hang so high in the nosebleeds that
the elephant rode in saddled and bearing up her boy

the cornerstone saw fit to sprout a flywheel and turn over.
All this happening is of proportion on reticulated vein-work.
When a thorn opens in the lake's soft side.
And once it's closed what's left are shallows and perennial.

OYSTER

A donkey brayed and an apple
fell from the sky. *Is this a joke?*
I said to the donkey. There we stood

blinking and stuck like darts to the hillside.
A worm poked out of the apple
and reared its body up and said telepathically

If it is then you're the butt of it
not him. Satisfied
I walked away before the sun

down the path my shadow laid. Which
by now was only nominally mine.
As he called the shots and told me where to go.

When we got there I knew where it was
because he knew it. And told me so by stopping.
It was the parking lot of abandoned K-Mart.

And we were alone under a streetlight.
And it was my birthday. And the sun was almost gone.
And one of us started humming.

ELI WHITNEY

They sky is tall and handsome
and lean as Eli Whitney. The river

is full of fish. Let me know
when it's time to be happy again.

MILLENNIUM

Look! Says the sun like a ripe old berry.
And just like that we all had something to talk about. Cruising along.
    Among
the wanton deck chairs. Amen. And the river

was time. And Jesse an understatement. An
unutterable force in chino pants. *Do you mark that?*
Says old St. John of Dreams. Plumbing the corners of the irises

and leaving no stone.
Make no mistake. It's only May. And not a whole new era. O John.
Snuff out your lamp with my forehead.

POSTSCRIPT

No more. No more tonight. Just as odd as it is thinking.
The radiator trails off midsentence. Danny chuffs up
all steam. Without a care in the world and giddy about
making arrangements. Back then we were baseball players. Thin

and smart in pants. Nobody knew what we had
hidden in our trunks. Tucked away in drawers. Space men. And
     brimming
cheek-high with Montgomery. Us two could've made a killing.
In one field or another. Okay. Do the good thing

says I. And good things'll follow. Ride out the lean times and be happy
when they're over. I was. And they were. We clapped
our hands. Somebody came back on stage. Clapped more
and they left. Then all of us left. Drove back home to fool around.

Hunter Grey is a Tennessee-born poet. He holds an MFA from the University of North Carolina Wilmington, and an MTS from Boston University. He and his wife currently live and work in Boston.

His work has previously appeared or is forthcoming in *Pigeon Pages, CUTTHROAT,* and *Pinch Online.*

This is his first chapbook.